4.81

DATE DUE

A
Patchwork,
Appliqué,
and
Quilting
Primer

A Patchwork, Appliqué, and Quilting Primer

Elyse Sommer
with Joellen Sommer

Illustrated by Giulio Maestro

Lothrop, Lee & Shepard Company | New York

Books by Elyse Sommer
Designing with Cutouts: The Art of Decoupage
Make It With Burlap
The Bread Dough Craft Book

Books by Joellen Sommer
Sew Your Own Accessories (with Elyse Sommer)

Printed in the United States of America.

1   2   3   4   5   79   78   77   76   75

Library of Congress Cataloging in Publication Data

Sommer, Elyse.
    A patchwork, appliqué, and quilting primer.
    Bibliography: p.
    SUMMARY: Basic instructions for developing skills in patchwork, appliqué, and quilting with a number of learn-by-doing projects for each technique.
    1. Patchwork—Juvenile literature.   2. Quilting—Juvenile literature.
3. Applique—Juvenile literature.
[1. Patchwork.   2. Quilting.   3. Applique.   4. Handicraft]
I. Sommer, Joellen, joint author.   II. Maestro, Giulio, ill.   III. Title.
TT835.S63   746.4'6   74-34152
ISBN 0-688-41693-4
ISBN 0-688-51693-9 lib. bdg.

To Joellen

She gave me the courage and incentive to try sewing after years of being a confirmed "non-sewer"

To Elyse

She gave me the courage to write up some of my ideas after years of being a confirmed "non-writer"

Our special thanks to Josie McKinley, whose quilting bees add a sense of community to our own Long Island neighborhood; and to Jane Golden, whose efforts on behalf of the New York Bi-Centennial have helped to bring a sense of neighborhood to the Greater New York area.

We'd also like to express our appreciation to the Hallmark Gallery for making available photos from their patchwork exhibit and to the America-Israel Cultural Foundation, Inc. for allowing us to photograph the work of Shulamit Litan.

A very special thanks to three young models; Andy, Jane, and Lucy Goetz.

Contents

This "Schoolhouse" quilt from the collection of Blanche Greenstein and Tom Woodard is an example of a nineteenth-century friendship or album quilt. It was probably intended as a gift for a friend moving away.

Photo courtesy of Hallmark Gallery

Introduction:
A New Look at
Traditional Crafts

If you like puzzles, you'll love the mathematical challenge of fitting shapes together to make a patchwork. If you prefer to work in a freer, less mathematically exact way, you'll love appliqué. If you can do a basic running stitch, you can quilt your patchwork and/or your appliqués, giving them additional texture and design, as well as warmth.

Before we begin our own adventure with patchwork, appliqué, and quilting, let's take a quick trip back in time so that we can better understand the differences and similarities between these crafts.

Quilting was the first of the three to become a widespread art. It was introduced on the European continent late in the eleventh century by the Crusaders, who discovered it in the Middle East. Like all crafts, quilting was born out of necessity; in this case, the necessity of protecting the body against extremes of climates. By stitching layers of fabric together and forming little air pockets between the stitches, the original quilters invented one of the simplest and earliest methods of insulation. After the Crusaders brought back what they had learned about techniques, shown in their quilted tunics and banners, the art of quilting spread all over Europe. By the time people began to migrate to America, quilting was an established craft and,

9

of course, the early settlers brought their quilts and their quilting skills with them. The designs on these early quilts were made only with stitches.

Patched fabrics for clothing have been traced back to earliest Egyptian times. However, it was in America that the quilt first became associated with patchwork. Here again, necessity was the first step towards creation. Life in America was hard. Cloth for new quilts or clothing was often impossible to obtain, and, when it could be bought, it was enormously expensive. Quilt tops were patched, and patched again. If new cloth was bought to make new clothing, every little snippet was saved and used. Eventually women learned to patch and piece in patterns which were beautiful as well as useful. The pieced patchwork was the result.

As times got better and fabrics were easier to come by, women continued to make patchwork quilts, for by this time what had started out of need had become pleasure as well. Now they were able to make their designs more interesting by the addition of cut-out patterns sewn on top of the patchwork. This applied or "laid on" work also has a long history. Applied lace work was practiced from the thirteenth century on in India and Persia, where it was probably invented. Applied work was also done in Italy, Germany, France, and England and eventually referred to any type of textile material sewn to another. The name appliqué is a French word which in turn is derived from the Latin word applicane, meaning to join or attach.

At the time the American patchwork story was developing, French needlewomen were especially well known for their appliqué skills and it was from them that the American quilters probably borrowed the technique. With the addition of appliqué, the quilts became stitched stories of the events in the lives of the quilters and their families. Parties known as quilting bees soon became popular social events. Here patterns and ideas were swapped back and forth. Quilts were finished around the quilting frame and future quilts were planned.

In this book we have presented traditional as well as modern methods for patchwork, appliqué, and quilting. The sample projects are small. Many are equal to one part or one block of a full-sized quilt. They are designed to be used and enjoyed as part of our present-day life styles. The very fact that patchwork, appliqué, and quilting are so adaptable to designs smaller and different from the traditional quilt add to their effectiveness as pleasurable and useful endeavors.

Once you've sampled the illustrated projects you may wish to make something really big, something you design yourself. That's where it's really at with any craft—whether you work big or small, the idea is to become familiar enough with the basics so that you can go on to create your own visions and fantasies.

Materials and Tools

Fabrics

Old-time patchworkers always worked with cotton. It has a smooth weave which makes it easy to pin and to sew, non-fraying edges, and great durability. The cottons today have the added benefits of being pre-shrunk, color-fast and best of all, permanent press. What's more, the choice of colors and prints in cotton and cotton blend fabrics is fantastic. You will have no problem finding everything you could want for great patchwork designs amidst the chintzes, denims, calicoes, ginghams, broadcloths, percales and muslins which make up the cotton family. Cotton blends such as cotton-dacron are great, but stay away from synthetics, rayons, or stretchy knits, which are hard to handle. Other fabrics are appealing because they have interesting textures; for example, velvet or silk. They're fine to use but a little harder to sew, so save them for later. Lightweight cotton corduroy has a nice texture and is still in the easy-to-use category.

The big question about fabric, of course, is old versus new. After all, didn't patchwork get started with the thrifty use of old scraps? It did, and you CAN use old materials by cutting apart discarded clothing, slipcovers, curtains, etc. However, once again, our advice is to do that later, and start with new fabric since it IS easier to work with. This doesn't mean you have to spend a lot of money. Don't forget you don't need much of any fabric so rummage through the remnant tables. If you have friends and relatives who sew, ask them to save their scraps for you. Their throw-aways may be the beginning of your newest patchwork.

A fabric not yet mentioned but well worth considering and using is felt. Felt is a pressed rather than a woven fabric. This means that the fabric edges won't fray when cut so that felt can be finished on its CUTTING edge. Felt is good as a backing, for appliqués, and any time you don't want to bother with seam allowances.

Scissors

You will need a pair of fabric shears, a pair for cutting paper, plus small embroidery scissors for cutting threads. Never use fabric scissors to cut paper since this will dull them.

Pins

Have lots of pins handy on a pincushion or in a covered box. Pin everything before sewing. Careful pinning can save basting.

Needles

Get an assortment of sewing needles—some short ones, some long ones, some with small threading eyes and some wide-eyed embroidery kinds. Quilting needles are some-what shorter and stouter than regular needles and can be found at regular notions counters.

Thread

Mercerized cotton thread is an all-purpose thread and will serve most of your sewing needs. For decorative stitchery, use embroidery thread or yarn.

Rulers

An ordinary wooden ruler is fine for measuring fabrics; for making and measuring templates you should also have a metal hard-edged ruler. Don't use a super-long yardstick for your fabric measuring. It will get in the way.

Cardboard, Matboard, Masonite, Balsa Wood, Sandpaper

Any of these materials are suitable for making templates or patterns. Flattened plastic from bleach bottles is an alternative to balsa wood.

X-Acto Knife or Single-Edged Razor Blades

When making templates known as window templates, the cardboard or balsa wood must be cut with a knife or razor blade.

Carbon and Tracing Paper

For tracing designs onto cardboard.

Pencils, Tailor's Chalk, Colored Markers

You'll need pencils to trace designs onto light fabrics and chalk for tracing them to darker fabrics. The colored mark-

14

ers are important when you are planning a design on paper to help you visualize the color effects of the design.

Graph Paper
Graph paper is an invaluable aid in drawing accurate shapes and for enlarging or reducing a design. For example, if a four-inch square is drawn on graph paper so that each square represents an inch, you can double the square by reproducing it on another sheet of graph paper where two squares are used to equal an inch.

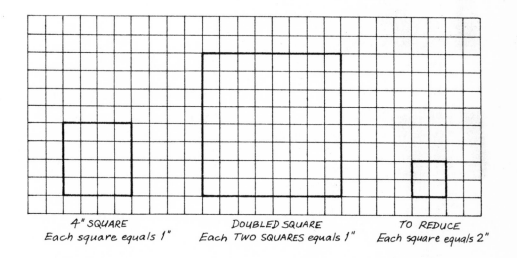

4" SQUARE
Each square equals 1"

DOUBLED SQUARE
Each TWO SQUARES equals 1"

TO REDUCE
Each square equals 2"

Newsprint
Large sheets of paper are needed to work out patterns and designs. Ordinary newspaper can be used. Just use dark markers so the lines will show through the print.

15

Stuffing Materials

Rolls of quilt batting are available from quilt suppliers (see Sources of Supplies) in both cotton and dacron. Cotton might be a bit cheaper but dacron is worth the extra money. Old blankets and mattress pads can be used instead of batting. For stuffed appliqués you can use wool scraps, dacron stuffing, or polyester stuffing. A good "free" stuffing is the lint that accumulates in the drier. This is a great fire hazard if not removed regularly so you'll be keeping your house safe if you check the lint accumulation regularly. If you keep it in a plastic bag, you'll be amazed how fast the bag will fill up.

Iron

Pressing seams of sewn patches is a must. A steam iron is helpful but if you don't have one, use a damp cloth between your iron and the article you press.

Sewing Machine

This is strictly optional. Every project included in this book can be made by hand. A sewing machine is a great time-saver, of course. Machine-sewn stitches are strong and firm. You can even embroider with a machine if you know how to use it. Even if you do use a machine, you'll probably want to do some things by hand. Many modern patchworkers mix hand and machine sewing depending on the projects, the mood, and their life-styles. Machine sewing may seem more modern because it's faster, but it isn't portable and modern life-styles don't keep us at home as much as old-fashioned ones. Our hobbies tend to be on the go with us—to picnics, beaches, on trips.

Zippers

Zippers are available in a wide assortment of colors and sizes. You will be using zippers for bag closings and for pillows if you want the pillow cover to be removable. Velcro is an even more modern and easier type of closing to use than a zipper. It consists of two pieces of tape that lock together when they are pressed between the fingers. They pull apart with a flick of the forefinger.

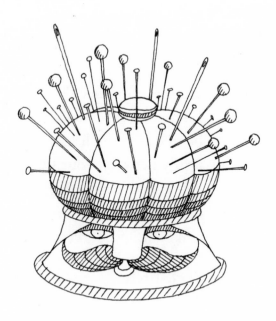

Basic Skills

STITCHES

You don't need any advanced sewing or embroidery skills to be good at patchworking, appliquéing, or quilting. Following are descriptions of three sewing stitches which will see you through all the projects in this book. Since it's fun to know a few extras too, these are followed by some simple embroidery stitches which will help you to add decorative touches to your work.

Running Stitch

Running Stitch

To make this truly all-purpose stitch, start from the underside of the fabric and pass the needle in and out of the fabric several times. Each stitch should be about ⅛ inch long. Hold the fabric firmly between your thumb and forefinger as you work. Running stitches can be used for decorative purposes, to make circles, curves, and other shapes.

Backstitch

This strong stitch is the same as the basic stitch made by a sewing machine.

18

Bring your thread through from the underside of the fabric on the stitch line. Take a small backward stitch, still on the stitch line, and bring the needle up again, leaving a small space between the first stitch and the point at which you bring up the needle. Then take another backward stitch to fill in the space.

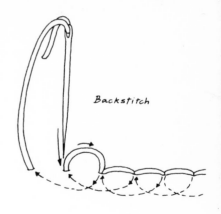

Backstitch

Overhand or Overlap Stitch

This is a slanting stitch that is excellent for joining one fabric, such as an appliqué, to another. Pin under your raw edges. Place the needle at right angles to the fabric and push it through the fabric from the back of the work to the front. The overhand stitch should again be small (⅛ inch). Take the needle to the back again and push through the front. The thread will curve over the edge of the joined fabrics. Keep your stitches very close together and be careful not to pull the thread too tight.

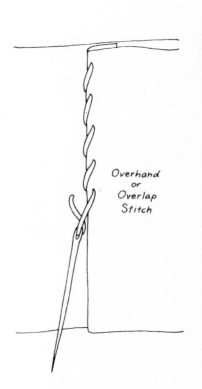

Overhand or Overlap Stitch

Blanket Stitch

This is similar to the overhand stitch, but more decorative. When joining two

19

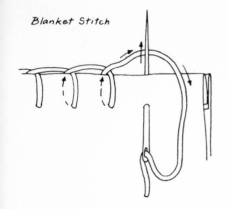

Blanket Stitch

pieces of fabric together on the right side with your joining stitch showing, use the blanket stitch. Make the same ⅛ inch stitch at the edge of the fabric, but straight up and down, instead of slanted. Before pulling the thread tight, weave the needle under the loop.

French Knot

Use this whenever you think a dot would add to your design. Bring your needle up at the top of the fabric. Wrap the thread around the needle two times. Bring the point of the needle back into the fabric, right next to the spot where you began. Pull needle and thread through. The double wrap will become knotted to the base.

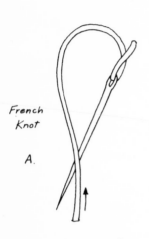

French Knot

A.

B.

C.

Fern Stitch

Pull your needle up through the fabric and make a straight stitch. Return the needle to the point at which you started and make another stitch a short distance from the first. Repeat this with the third stitch. All stitches should be the same length.

Fern Stitch

Cross Stitch

Insert the needle from the underside of the fabric to the top and make a diagonal stitch from A to B. Come out at C and go up to D. Go down the row and then come back to complete the crosses.

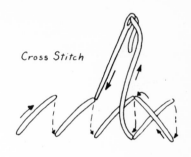

Cross Stitch

Satin Stitch

This is a straight stitch worked across a shape or pattern to fill it in. The stitches can be vertical, horizontal, regular or irregular.

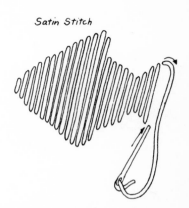

Satin Stitch

Seeding Stitch

This is really a stitch pattern more than a stitch. Make very small straight stitches, straight or at angles; next to each other, or on top of each other.

Seeding Stitch

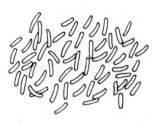

Patchwork Techniques

Cutting out patches and joining them together is no more complicated than the basic sewing stitches. The watchword here is accuracy. In order for two shapes to line up alongside each other, they must be cut out accurately. In order to keep the fabric from unraveling, stitches must be made a little inside of the edge. Therefore your patches must be cut to allow for the extra space called the seam allowance.

Templates

The surest way to have accurately cut patches is to use a pattern or template as a guide. The template is outlined onto the fabric before cutting is done.

Draw the shape you want on graph paper. This will help you to get everything even. There are a number of basic geometric patterns in this book and you can start out by tracing these and using them as your template patterns. Before the pattern is ready to be made into a

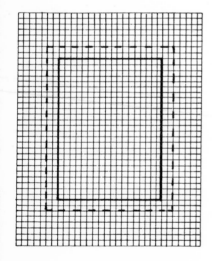

template, you must draw in a seam allowance line. To do this, draw a series of dots or dashes ¼″ outside the pattern line. Some patchworkers prefer a wider ⅜″ seam allowance and this is fine too. We will refer to the seam allowance as one measuring ¼″ throughout the book.

You can make two types of templates:

1. Glue your paper pattern to cardboard, posterboard or the smooth side of sandpaper. Use just a dab of glue, a bit of double-sided Scotch tape or gluestick. Cut around the paper pattern along the dots or dashes. Be sure to use your paper scissors. You now have a template the exact size of your patch, INCLUDING the seam margin.

2. Trace your paper pattern to the template material, outlining both the actual size of the patch and the seam allowance. With an X-Acto knife or a single-edged razor blade held against a metal-edged ruler, cut out both the inside and the outside of the pattern. You now have what is called a window template.

The advantage of the window tem-

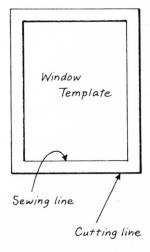

Window
Template

Sewing line

Cutting line

23

plate is that it allows you to draw the sewing AND the cutting line onto your fabric quickly and accurately. We feel that in the long run, especially for hand sewing, this extra effort will pay off.

Permanent Templates

Cardboard templates will eventually get worn and frayed. It pays to consider making your templates in materials which will hold up well. Old-time patch-workers used to take their patterns to the local tinsmith who would cut them out in metal. If you have a friend with a jigsaw, you could buy some Masonite and ask him or her to cut some patterns out of that. You can also make inex-pensive and permanent sort of patterns of balsa wood. This can be cut with an X-Acto knife. A good ecological idea is to use plastic from discarded items such as bleach bottles. Cut the bottles into pieces and soak in warm water to flatten.

Appliqué Templates

If you use templates for appliqué de-signs, accuracy is not as important as when you piece patches to make fabric.

Just draw or trace your design onto
cardboard, then cut the fabric some-
what larger to allow an edge which will
be tucked under at random. Cut some
notches all around the design to make
the tucking easier.

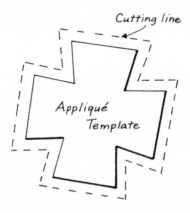

Cutting line

Appliqué
Template

Cutting Out

Place your template on the WRONG
side of the fabric. Outline with pencil
on light fabric, with tailor's chalk on
dark fabric. If you use a window template you will be outlining both the inside and the outside portions so that
your sewing as well as your cutting line
is clearly marked on the fabric—the
seam line is estimated as you sew. Be
sure to cut fabric with fabric scissors.

25

Joining Patches

Pin patches to be joined with the right sides of the fabrics against each other (see sketch). Make a running or backstitch along the seam line, ¼″ from the edge of the fabric. Open your sewn patch and press the seam to one side. Do not press the seams open as is usual with other types of sewing.

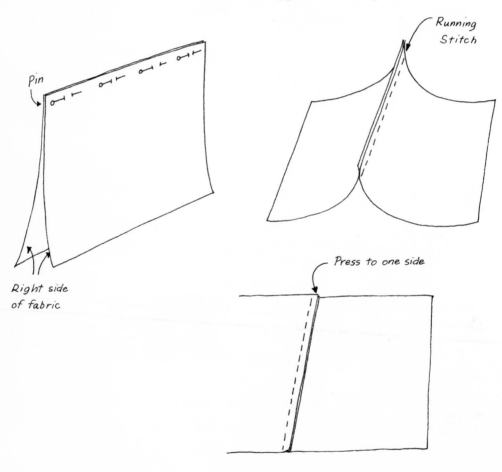

Pin

Running Stitch

Right side of fabric

Press to one side

Designing

Random Squares

The simplest designs are those where patches of fabric are made by piecing squares, all of the same size, without any special color or fabric pattern. No fabric or print needs to be repeated. The design pattern which results from this random patching is always a delightful surprise.

Squares-and-Rectangles-in-a-Row

The random joining of squares into rows of patchwork fabric can be changed by alternating squares with rectangles. The rectangles can be in different widths, from narrow strips to two or three times the length of a square. The height of all the pieces should be the same. Since this type of patching results in a pattern of shapes, it is not necessary to use a lot of different prints.

An amazing number of pattern variations are possible by combining squares and rectangles of different widths.

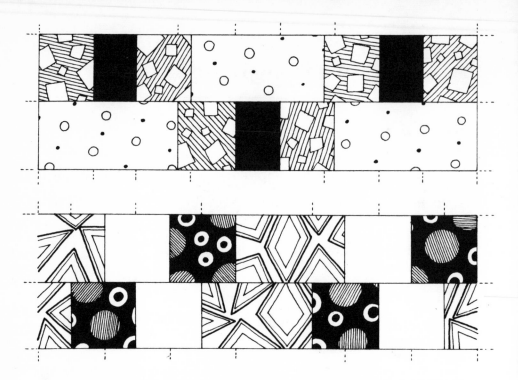

Using Color to Create Patterns

By using groups of one type of print or color in combination with others, definite patterns and shapes will emerge. In a design of squares, for example, you can use an equal number of squares in two fabrics and alternate one with the other. The result is a checkerboard design. By using the same shapes, but making all the border squares one color and only the middle square a contrasting color, a completely different pattern emerges.

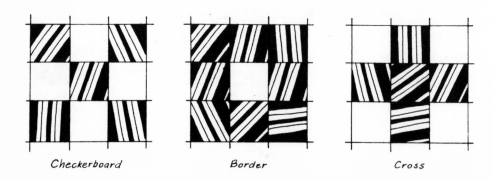

Checkerboard   Border   Cross

Mixed Geometrics

The range of your designs can be increased to the point of infinity by designing with other geometric shapes. Triangles, diamonds, hexagons and even pentagons are as popular with patchwork designers as squares. The shapes are simple to cut and to fit together. Combining the shapes, or using shapes of different sizes in one design leads to still more variation. Once you start working with geometric shapes you will understand why they have been used in architecture, mosaic making and wood parquetry throughout history. When all possible combinations seem to have been tried, new possibilities develop.

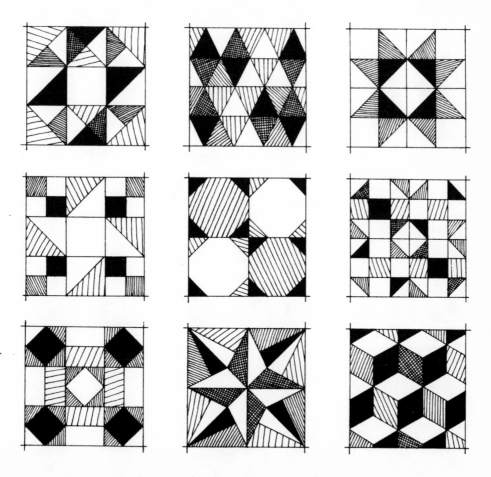

✗ Crazy Quilt Design

A crazy quilt design is like a mosaic. Patches of random size, shape, and color are combined without particular pattern plan.

Learn-by-Doing
Patchwork Projects

Random Square and Rectangle Belt

It would take more of these belts than we could count to make up a traditional patchwork quilt. That's why this quick patchwork project is such a great way to get started. By the time you make one for yourself and everyone on your gift-giving list, you'll be an experienced patchworker.

Materials:

Solid piece of backing fabric in a color that will contrast well with the patches you use since it will show when the belt is pulled through the loop. The fabric should be 2½" wide. To determine the amount you will need for the length, measure your waist or hips, depending on where you wear your belts, and add 4 inches to this. For instance, if your waist is 22 inches, your backing fabric should measure 2½" by 26".

2½" square patches of printed cotton, plus scraps cut into rectangles ranging from 2½" by ¾" to 2½" by 3".

One set of metal belt loops.

How to Make It:

1. Place your patches in a pleasing arrangement of color and shapes. Lay them out in a row, with seam allowances

31

overlapped, right beneath the solid backing fabric. That way you will be sure to allow for the seams being sewn together and will avoid the possibility of having the patched fabric shorter than the backing fabric.

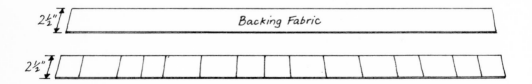

2. Pin-baste patch #1 and patch #2, right sides facing. Sew together along seam line with backstitch.
3. Sew the third patch to the sewn-together patch #1-2.
4. Keep adding patches until the top of your belt is pieced together.
5. Iron all the seams to one side.

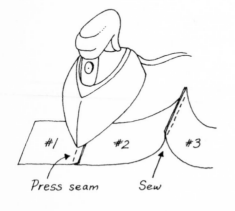

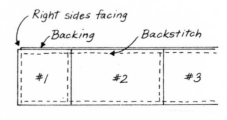

6. Pin the patched fabric and the backing fabric right sides together. Backstitch along the seam allowance of three sides, leaving one short side open.

7. Turn the belt right side out through the OPEN end. Use a long ruler to help push it through. Sew the open end together with an overhand stitch.

8. Slip one end of the belt through both belt loops and backstitch in place. Make three rows of stitches to secure the loops.

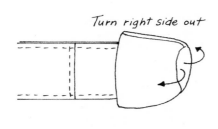

Turn right side out

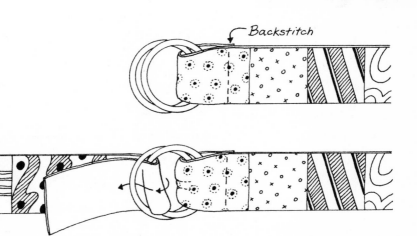

Backstitch

Double-Sided
Nine-Patch Pillow

Each side of this pillow will be assembled as a separate block measuring 12″ square and made up of nine pieced patches. This is called a nine-patch in patchwork language.

Materials:

4 pieces of fabrics in prints, solid colors, or a combination of both. You will need a 20″ square from each of three fabrics and a 30″ square from the fourth.

Stuffing—polyester or foam are ideal for pillows; the amount depends upon the desired amount of fullness.

How to Make It:

1. Make a template using the pattern as your guide (see sketch).

2. Cut out five patches in color A, four patches in color B, three patches in color C, and six patches in color D. Colors A and B will be used for the checkerboard side; colors C and D will be used for side two which is called a "Jacob's Ladder" design.

3. Lay out your color A and B patches to match the checkerboard pattern (see sketch). With a running or backstitch, sew one row of three patches at a time. Then sew row 2 to row 1 and row 3 to rows 1-2 as indicated in the sketch on page 36.

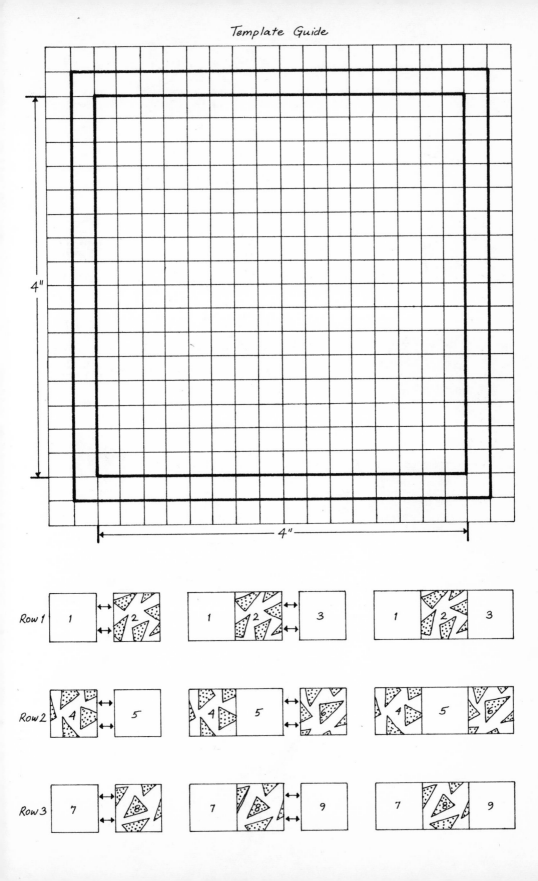

Template Guide

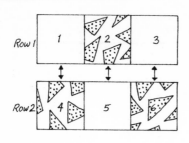

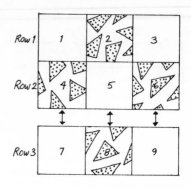

4. Lay out the remaining nine patches to match the diagram for side two and sew together in rows as indicated in the sketch.

5. To make your two blocks into a pillow, pin the two patched squares, right sides together. Backstitch three sides and turn inside out. Stuff and sew the last side with overhand stitches.

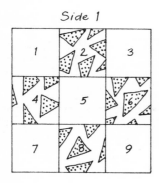

Side 1

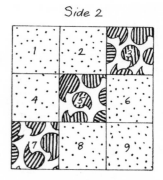

Side 2

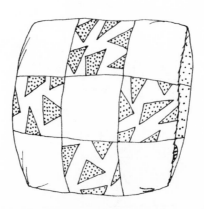

To make a large floor pillow, make four nine-patch blocks for each side. To make each side of the pillow, sew two of the nine-patch blocks together to make row 1. Sew together two more and sew this row to the first. Your pillow top is now a four-patch pattern. The overall dimensions are 24 inches by 24 inches.

You could make all your blocks the same, but this would be a good chance to practice the combination of blocks. To get more variety into your design, use three fabrics instead of two for each block and then move your prints around to create different pattern effects (see sketch.)

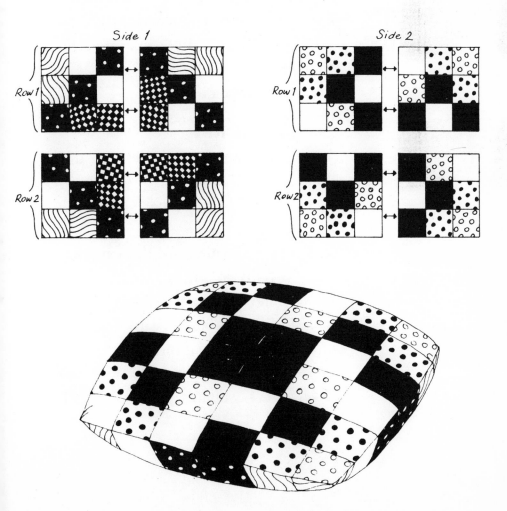

Patch-Pocket
Tote Bag

The patch-pocket adds pizzazz to this roomy tote bag and introduces you to a right angle triangle and its infinite design possibilities.

Materials:

Denim, sailcloth or similar sturdy fabric, 20½″ by 20½″

One dark and one light print, 10½″ by 20½″ each; these will be cut into eight triangles each.

Decorative rope or cord

How to Make It:

1. Cut a template to match the diagram.

2. Cut out eight triangles, four in each color.

3. Pin two triangles, one in each print, with the right sides facing together (see sketch) and sew along the seam line or long side of the triangles with a running or backstitch. Repeat three times.

4. Iron all seams to one side. You now have four 4″ squares pieced from triangles.

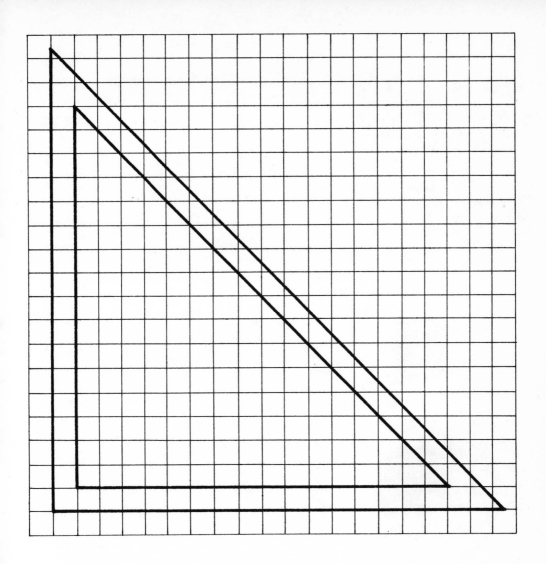

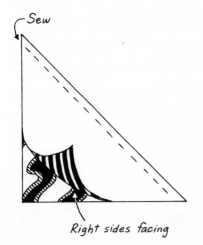

Sew

Right sides facing

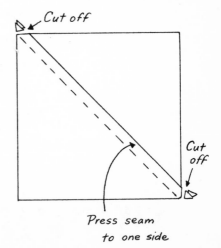

Cut off

Cut off

Press seam
to one side

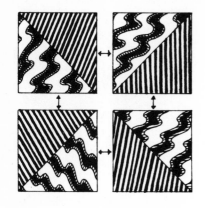

5. Lay out the four triangle-pieced squares to make the pinwheel design as shown in the sketch. Sew together in rows of two patches each.

6. Pin the pocket to the center of the top half of the 20½ by 20½ inch bag fabric. The wrong side of the pocket should face the right side of the bag fabric.

7. Sew the pocket down at the sides and bottom with a running or overhand stitch. Leave the top of the pocket open, but tuck under and sew down the edge to prevent fraying.

8. Fold the bag in half with the right sides (including the patch-pocket) facing inward. Backstitch at both sides, and turn right side out again.

9. Sew rope handle in place, leaving an inch or two loose at the bottom for a fringed effect (see sketch).

If you have extra fabric you can make a patchwork handle, following the instructions for the random square and rectangle belt project. Use the bag fabric as your backing. You can now make a more interesting design than you did for the belt by patching tri-

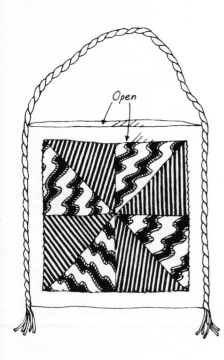

Open

Patchwork Handle

angles together to make some of the squares (see sketch.)

Here are some other ways you might arrange your triangle designs to make the patch pockets, using the same size template:

1.

2 Print Variation

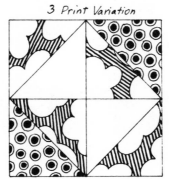

3 Print Variation

2. Star

Now that you know how to work with pieced triangles as well as squares, you might want to make another nine-patch pillow, combining the shapes.

The addition of triangles gives a new look to the same basic pattern—see sketch #1.

The addition of triangles to squares results in a four-pointed star—see sketch #2.

Another square and triangle combination results in a design known as the "Shoo-Fly"—see sketch #3.

3. Shoo-Fly

41

All kinds of pictures can be created with mixed geometric shapes. Eighteen fabric patches arranged in a pattern of dark and light squares and triangles will result in a sailboat design (see sketch.)

Linda Goldman, a young contemporary patchworker, uses a combination of shapes to create her charming "House on

"House on the Hill" pillow top design by Linda Goldman of Warwick, New York. *Photo by P. David Horton.*

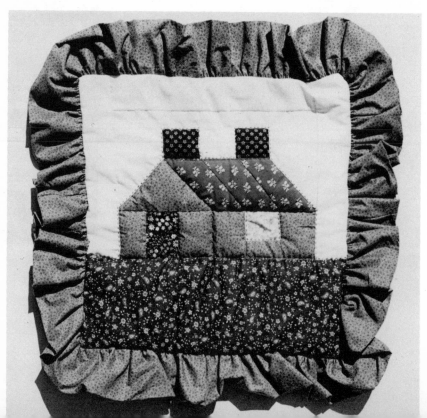

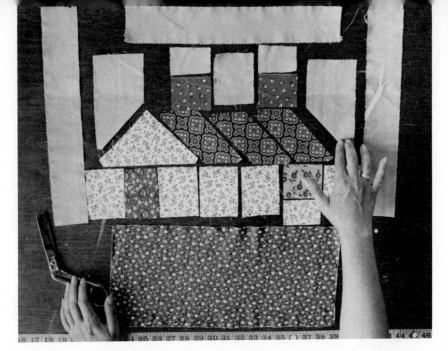

Patches for "House on the Hill" laid out for patching and sewing.

the Hill" pillow tops. If you look at the photo with the pieces laid out for sewing you will see that you can cut larger patches made up of several shapes. The slanted roof is in the shape of a parallelogram. A parallelogram pattern can be made by drawing four equilateral triangles, turned top to bottom to form a row (see sketch).

Parallelogram

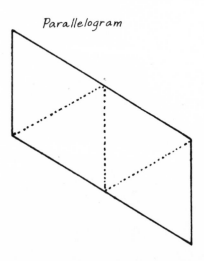

Isosceles Triangle Halter

The isosceles triangle is an excellent addition to your collection of patchwork shapes. This easy-to-make halter, which could fit anyone from six to about twelve, illustrates how well this triangle combines to make other shapes.

Materials:

Four prints were used to make the samples: 10½″ squares in 3 prints, each of which will be cut to make two triangles; ⅓ yard of the fourth fabric will make the other two triangles plus a lining.
1 yard of ribbon, lace, or bias cord for halter ties.

How to Make It:

1. Make a template using the diagram as a guide.
2. Cut out eight fabric patches, two in each print.
3. Lay out the patches to match the sketch.

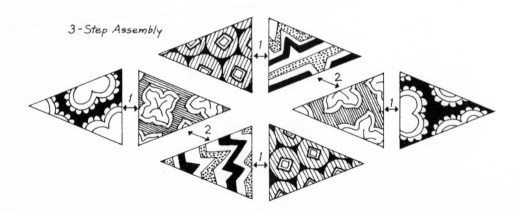

3-Step Assembly

Template Guide

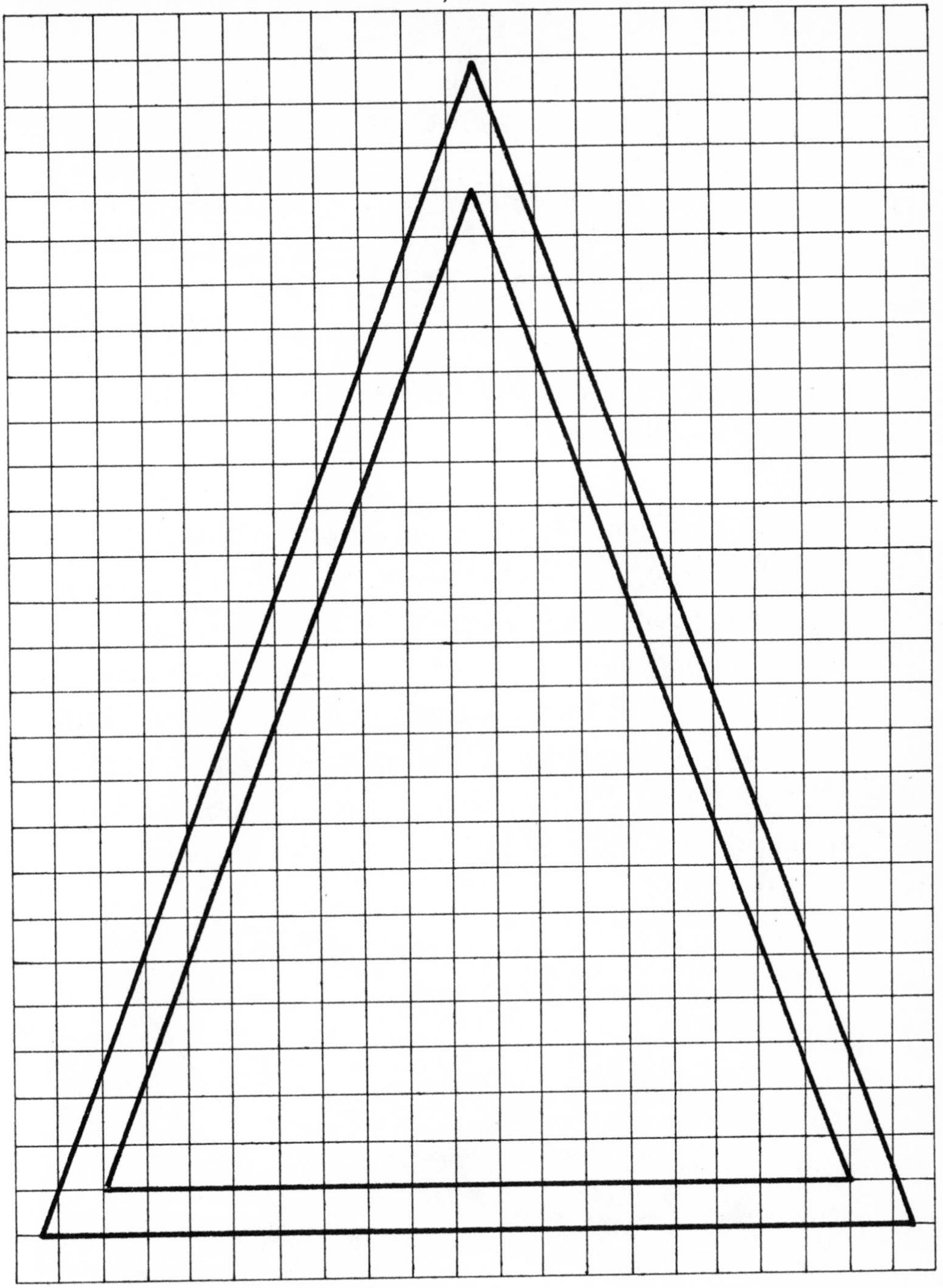

4. Pin the patches in pairs to form diamonds. With a running or backhand stitch, sew each set of triangles together, right sides facing.

5. Join the diamonds in rows as shown in the sketch. You will have a large patched diamond.

6. Pin the completed patchwork to the left-over print and cut all around, allowing ¼″ extra for the seam allowance.

7. Pin the patched and solid pieces, right sides facing. With a running or backstitch, sew together, leaving an opening to push right sides out. After you have turned the fabric right side out, finish sewing with overhand stitches.

Ties

Reverse side

8. Sew ribbon ties to the center of the halter and at each side point. The finished halter is reversible.

Isosceles Triangle Halter. Joellen Sommer, designer-sewer.

Diamond Patch
Pajama Bag

Diamonds are all-time favorites with patchworkers. Traditional quiltmakers have at times pieced together THOUSANDS of tiny diamonds to make up bed-sized quilts.

Materials:

Dark and light print, ⅓ yard each
4½″ × 8½″ patch for flesh-colored diamonds
7-9″ zipper or velcro
⅓ yard decorative cord
Scrap wool for hair stitchery
Felt, buttons, waterproof permanent markers or paint for facial trim

How to Make It:

1. Make one diamond template and one half-diamond template using the patterns as guides.
2. Cut two flesh-colored diamond patches, four light print diamond patches, six dark print patches, and eight light print half diamond patches. Divide the patches in half and put one set aside.
3. Embroider, draw, or appliqué buttons or felt scraps to one of the flesh-colored patches to make the doll's face. Stitch bits of scrap wool in place for hair.

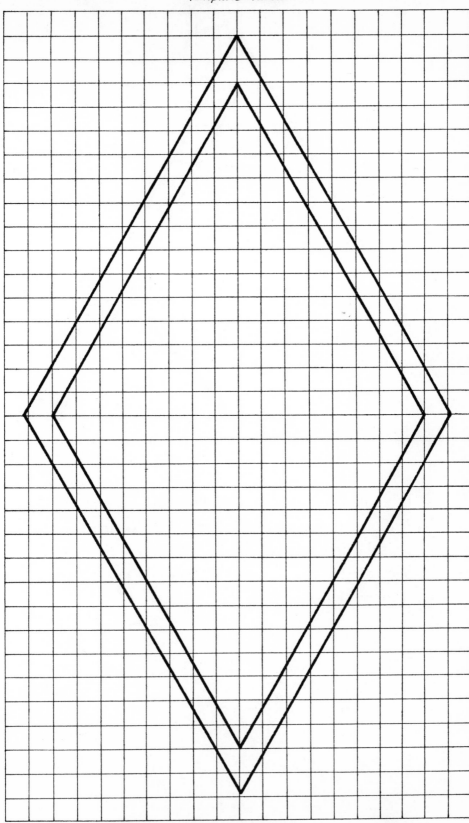

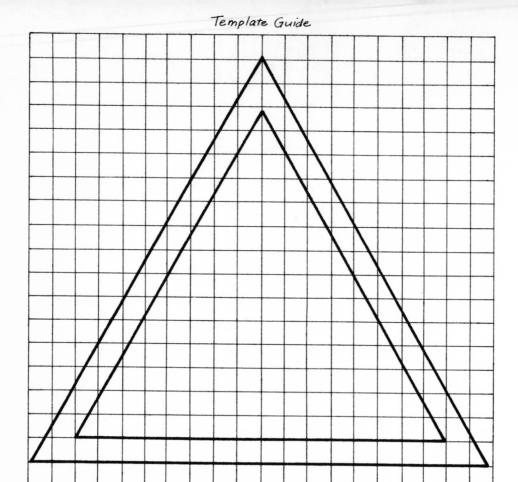

4. Lay out your patches to follow the pattern. Pin and backstitch into rows as indicated on the sketch. The face patch is the first patch of row 1.

5. Sew row 2 to row 1, row 3 to rows 1-2. The last triangle marked row 4 goes on last.

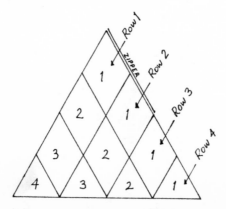

6. Prepare the patches for the back. Cover the remaining flesh-colored patch with wool hair. Then sew everything together exactly as you did the front; the wool-covered head patch first, and so on.

7. Place the two large triangles with the right sides facing in. With a running or backstitch, sew along the seam line around all three sides leaving open the part where you want the zipper or velcro closing to go. Sew the zipper in place and turn the bag right side out.

8. Sew decorative cord to each side of the head for hanging and carrying.

Now that you've made your first diamond patchwork project, get out your graph paper and colored pencil and try making some other diamond designs. See what happens when you place two diamonds next to each other, and then draw one on top of them. Color the block to the left a medium color, the next one a very dark color. Leave the top light. This is known as a diamond Baby Block.

Draw diamonds into a star pattern.

Diamond Baby Blocks

Diamond Star

A spectacularly beautiful example of one of the all-time favorite diamond designs—*The Star of Bethlehem*. From the collection of Blanche Greenstein and Tom Woodard. *Photo courtesy of Hallmark Gallery*

Hexagon Cat Rattle

The hexagon is a lovely shape. This baby rattle combines short and long hexagons. This design can also become a wall ornament by adding loops between the cat's ears.

Materials:

Two prints, a 12″ square of each, to make two patches for each pattern
Felt scraps for eyes, ears, and whiskers
Stuffing—scrap wool or lint
Small box with fitted cover
Some pebbles

How to Make It:

1. Make a template for the two hexagons and cut two patches for each one. Use the pattern as your guide.
2. Copy the ear pattern and cut out four felt shapes to match. Sew two pieces together with overhand or running stitches at sides A and B. Stuff lightly and lay aside.

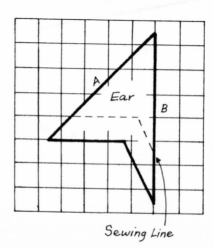

Sewing Line

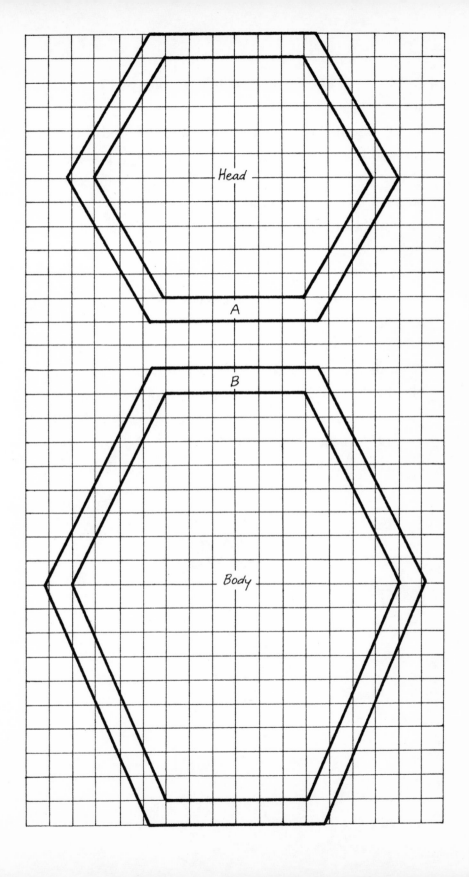

3. Sew eyes and whisker details to one of the head hexagons.

4. Pin the hexagon face to the hexagon body so that the parts of the pattern marked A and B join. The right sides should be facing in. Backstitch along the seam line and repeat for the other two pieces.

5. Pin the front and the back of the cat together with the right sides facing in. Pin the ears in place so they can be sewn right in.

6. Backstitch all around the cat's body but leave the bottom open.

7. Turn the cat inside out.

8. Stuff the cat lightly. Push the little box filled with pebbles in the middle of the stuffing. Finish sewing the cat's body together with overhand stitches.

9. Roll a piece of felt into the shape of a tail and sew or glue closed. Sew this to the bottom of the cat's body.

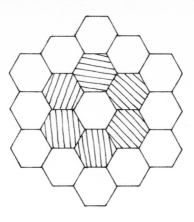

Use your colored pencils and paper to work out other hexagon designs. Surround a hexagon with a circle or circles of hexagons in other colors and you will see a lovely flower take shape.

A hexagonal quilt in the making. This is called "Grandmother's Flower Garden." Courtesy of Josie McKinley.

Appliqué

In recent years appliqué has been of great interest to artists who consider themselves fiber or fabric artists rather than patchworkers. Many are not even aware that they are working in the patchwork tradition. Modern appliqué includes stitchery, drawing and painting, as well as fabric sewing. Since landscapes seem to have great appeal for appliqué artists everywhere, let's see how a landscape would be handled in the pieced patchwork as well as the more free-form way.

Pieced Appliqué Landscape Hanging— "Moon-Over-the-Mountain"

Four patches—two for the triangular mountain and two for the round moon—are pieced to make a Moon-Over-the-Mountain landscape.

Materials:
12-inch felt square, light blue for background
9½-inch square of deep blue fabric for the sky
8-inch square of yellow fabric for two half moon patches
10-inch square of brown or green fabric for triangular mountain patches
Felt scraps or ribbons for hanging loops
Dowel stick

How to Make It:

1. Use the triangle pattern from the patch-pocket tote bag, page 39, for the mountain. Cut two patches of your mountain fabric to match.

2. Trace the half moon pattern (see sketch) two times on the back of the yellow fabric and cut out.

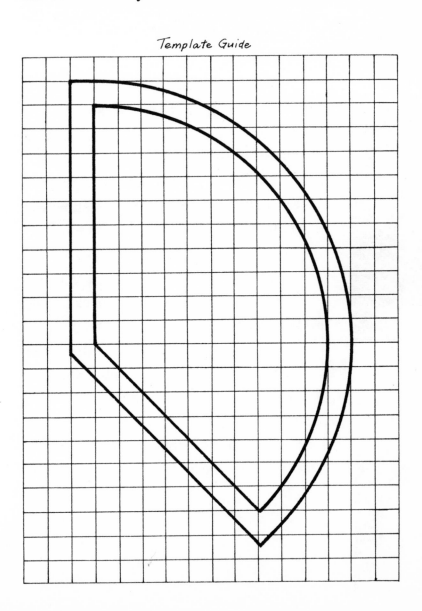

Template Guide

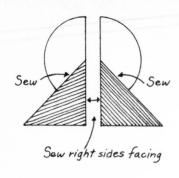

Sew — Sew

Sew right sides facing

Notch moon patches
to tuck
under

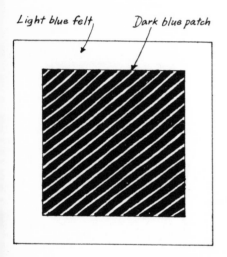

Light blue felt   Dark blue patch

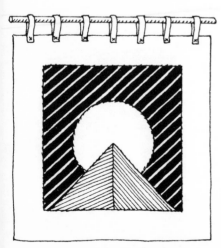

3. Backstitch one half moon patch to one half mountain patch as shown in the sketch. Repeat for the other two patches.

4. Place the two pieced patches together, right sides in and sew down the straight seam edge as shown in the sketch.

5. Open up the completed design and press all the seams to one side.

6. Cut little notches all around the moon so that the fabric can be tucked under when you sew.

7. Stitch the dark blue felt square to the light blue felt square as shown in pattern.

8. Pin the appliqué to the sky fabric, tucking under all the edges as you pin. Sew the appliqué to the sky background with running or overhand stitches.

9. Pin the appliquéd patch to the center of the dark blue felt square and sew in place with a decorative stitch such as the blanket or cross stitch.

10. Sew felt or ribbon loops to the top of the hanging and mount on the dowel.

60

Free-Form
Landscape Hanging

By changing the colors of the mountains and the sky fabric, you can make a series of these hangings, one for each season—a bright and sunny sky with green mountains for summer; gray sky with icy snow-covered mountains for winter; red sky with brown mountains for fall; yellow sky with mixed pastel-colored mountains for spring.

Materials:

Large sheets of newspaper or plain newsprint paper to make practice cuts of mountain ranges and to use as pattern guides for fabrics

Sky-colored felt, 12″ by 14½″ for the background (no seam allowance needed)

Two prints, 10″ by 14″ for large mountain ranges

One scrap print for small mountain range

One scrap of yellow for sun appliqué

Felt or ribbon scraps for hanging loop

Dowel

Optional: Felt in blue to contrast with sky background, 13″ by 15½″ to use as a backing for the hanging. The extra inch all around will serve as a border.

How to Make It:

1. Cut a piece of paper to match the felt background. Then cut mountain ranges free-form. You should have two which are as wide as the background. One could go about two-thirds up the background, the other somewhat lower. The third mountain will be small. Arrange the mountains so that the biggest is closest to the backing, the smallest on top of the others, but at the bottom of the hanging (see sketch). Cut other shapes until you have a design which pleases you.

2. Cut out a sun shape from yellow fabric. Be sure to make it large enough to cut notches which can be tucked under.

3. Lay each mountain range on the back of a print. Draw the outline onto your fabric free-form, being sure to add extra fabric to be tucked under. Cut out, making notches along the curves of the mountains for tucking under.

4. Pin the largest mountain range to the felt background.

5. Pin the second mountain on top of the first and the smallest on top of the middle one. Be sure to tuck and pin under the bottoms of all the mountains.

6. Pin the sun in place.

7. If you want an extra backing which will frame or border the hanging, center and pin the hanging to the largest blue felt fabric.

8. Sew everything down with running stitches, going through all the fabric layers at once.

9. Sew on loops and mount on dowel.

Sun:
Use circle
as
guide

Variations of the Landscape Appliqué Hanging

These landscape designs are very handsome when appliquéd to handbags.

By leaving the top of the mountains open, the landscapes can become useful as knick-knack holders. If you use your hanging as a catchall, it is advisable to line each mountain range for strength and a finished look. Just cut out each mountain range two times. Pin the two matching mountains, right sides facing in, and sew around top and sides, leaving the bottom unsewn. Turn the mountains right sides out and sew in place. No need to sew the bottoms together separately. All three can be folded under and stitched down together.

LEFT: Free-form landscape handbag. Joellen Sommer, designer-sewer.
RIGHT: When the tops of the mountains of an appliquéd landscape are left unsewn, it becomes a handy catchall hanging. Joellen Sommer, designer-sewer.

Pocketful of Stuffed Appliqué Daisies

Appliqués can be given an extra dimension by stuffing parts or all of the appliqué designs. A pocket of stuffed daisies would look good on pants, jackets, or shirts, for man, woman, or child. It could also be used as the first block in a whole quilt of different stuffed and appliquéd flower designs.

Materials:
5½" by 7½" material for pocket
Scraps of print fabric for flowers
Scraps of yellow for flower centers
Scraps of green for leaves
Green or brown bias tape or felt strips for flower stems
Small amount of stuffing—wool scraps, dacron, or polyester

How to Make It:
1. Fold down and sew the top seam edge of the pocket, with backstitch, running, or overhand stitch.
2. Cut flowers, flower centers, and

leaves free-form. Be sure to cut large enough for edges to be notched and turned under. If you use felt you can avoid seam edge and tucking.

3. Pin flowers, leaves, and stems in place. Stuff the leaves. Use running stitches to sew everything in place.

4. With overhand stitches, sew centers to the flowers, stuffing lightly as you sew.

5. Sew the pocket in place, also with overhand stitches, turning under the edges as you sew.

Reverse Appliqué Sun Patch

Appliqués can be made by layering two or three pieces of fabric and then cutting away areas from the top and middle layers, so that the underneath colors show through. This technique is called reverse appliqué and was perfected by the San Blas Indians. Done in the traditional manner, reverse appliqué (also known as molas) is difficult and time-consuming since each layer has to be cut, tucked under, and stitched separately. However, by working with felt, the reverse appliqué can be cut like paper and all the layers stitched at once.

Materials:
Three 7″ felt squares in different colors

How to Make It:
1. Use a small plate as a template to draw the circle outline of the patch. Then cut three felt circles to match.
2. Outline the points of the sun design near the outer edge of the felt circle you

plan to use on top (see sketch). Cut out the middle of the circle.

3. Pin this cut layer over the middle layer and pencil facial details onto the middle piece of felt.

4. Cut the details out of the second layer. Your scissors should have sharp points for this cutting. Start cutting in the middle areas and work out towards the edge.

5. Pin the two top layers to the bottom layer and baste the three layers together.

6. Sew all around the cut outlines with running stitches, going through all the layers of felt. Use embroidery thread.

7. Sew the patch to the background— a shirt or sweater, a patch of fabric for a hanging. Use a blanket stitch, overhand stitch, or other decorative stitch.

8. Remove basting stitches.

More Appliqué Design Ideas

Here are some other popular appliqué
motifs you might want to try either as
part of a large project or to give a new
look to a shirt or other item of clothing.

A very contemporary patchwork hanging, with stuffed appliqué and beading to add a three-dimensional quality. Artist Shulamit Litan. Photographed at the American-Israel Cultural Foundation.

Your own drawings can be used for appliqué inspiration. This appliquéd hanging was done in bright colors of red, green, and yellow against a blue sky. Artist Carole Irgo. *Photo courtesy of artist.*

✳ Quilting

Since we have already made a number of exciting patchwork and appliqué projects without quilting, you may have guessed that you can do patchwork and/or appliqué without quilting at all. The purpose of quilting is primarily to add a layer of warmth and the quilting process is a matter of firmly stitching this layer in place. However, quilting also adds textural beauty to your designs and, thanks to modern materials and methods, it need not be terribly time-consuming or difficult.

Selecting and Arranging Your Materials for Quilting

1. Quilt only pieces small enough to handle easily without large equipment. Even when you go beyond the small learn-by-doing projects, we would suggest that you quilt as you go along. Many modern quilters who make huge bed-sized coverings complete one block of the quilt before going on to the next.

2. Use only dacron batting. This does not need a lot of tiny stitches to hold its shape. At one time only cotton was available but unless held down with lots of stitches it will lump and shift around. That's why the old-time quilts all have such intricate quilting designs.

3. Avoid unnecessary finishing (known as binding off the quilt). Assemble your top, middle, and bottom layers with the finishing of the edge in mind. There are two easy ways to do this:

a. Make your middle layer smaller than the top and bottom. Tuck a half an inch of both top and bottom towards the inside as you do when you turn under an appliqué edge. Pin these edges securely all around. Sew around the edges with overhand stitches. Your quilt will be finished without the need of a border. What's more, it will be reversible.

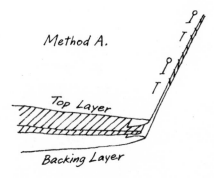

Method A.

Top Layer

Backing Layer

b. Cut either the top or backing layer one to three inches larger than the others. The edges of the larger layer can be folded to come up around the shorter one to form a border which can be sewn down as you quilt. In order to keep the

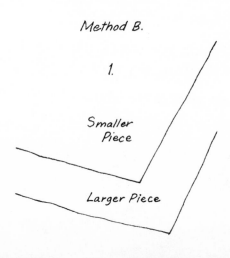

Method B.

1.

Smaller
Piece

Larger Piece

corners from bunching up, they should be mitered before folding up the edges. To do this, fold each corner towards the center so that it will form a small triangle(see sketch). Pin this triangle in place and **THEN** fold over the edges.

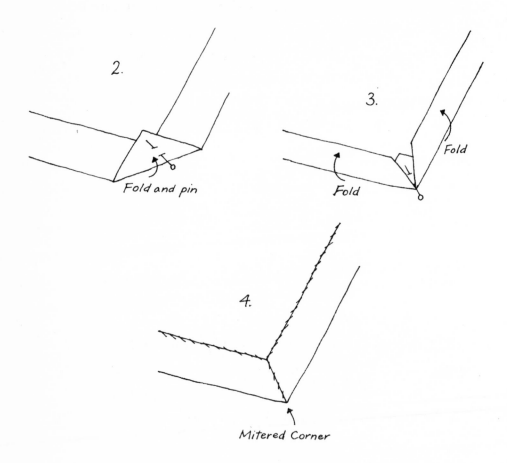

2.

Fold and pin

3.

Fold

Fold

4.

Mitered Corner

4. Always pin and baste your three layers together before sewing. This is not a step to skip in order to save time.
5. To hold your work while quilting, you can stretch it inside an embroidery hoop to keep it nice and taut. More and

more quilters have found that they can work comfortably without any kind of frame, especially with small-size patches. This gives you a chance to do quilting anywhere—while watching television, waiting for a dentist appointment, sitting at the beach or near a lake in the summer.

How to Quilt

Quilting is really no different from any other sewing. The quilting stitch is nothing more than a running stitch. Those who quilt in a frame or a hoop usually make their stitch straight up and down, half a stitch at a time. In other

Two twentieth century ladies in antique costumes demonstrated the art of quilting—both with a quilting frame and by hand (this is known as lap quilting)—at the "American Patchwork" mini-exhibit held at New York's Hallmark Gallery.   *Photo courtesy of Hallmark Gallery.*

words, they bring the needle up from the underside of the fabric, down from the top through to the back, and then back to the top in a second, separate motion. When you quilt in your lap, you can take several running stitches at once. It will take a bit to get used to pushing the needle through the extra layers of fabric. You will find a quilting needle, which is shorter than a regular needle, and quilting thread, helpful for this. Both are available in most notions departments.

Quilting Patterns

The pattern of your quilting stitches can be as simple as the stitch. The easiest way to quilt is simply to outline the patch and/or the appliqué design. When you made the reverse appliqué sun god patch you actually did outline quilting when you stitched around the cut features.

You can use quilting stitches to make a pattern in addition to the patchwork. A pattern of squares for example, can be covered with a criss-cross of quilt stitches (see sketch).

Cross Stitch Pattern

You can make round stitch patterns to offset the angles of a geometric design or to create colorless stitch patterns on solid areas of material.

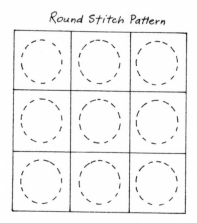

Round Stitch Pattern

TUFTING OR TYING A QUILT

This is a fast, easy, and decorative substitute sort of quilting. Thread an embroidery needle with two to four strands of yarn. Pass the threaded needle from the front of the patchwork through the back. Be sure to leave the loose ends of the threads on top. Bring the needle back up, close

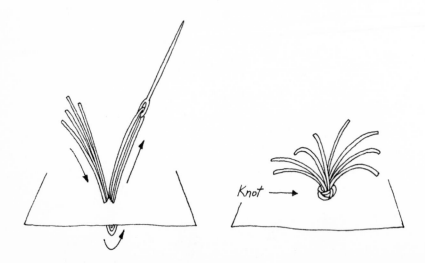

Knot →

to where you started. Take your needle off the thread. Make a tight knot with the loose threads and cut off, leaving a little tuft or fringe.

Now let's go back to two of our appliqué projects and see how they would be quilted. . .

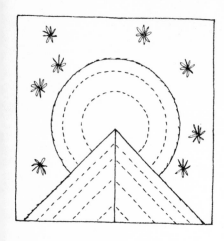

Quilting and Tufting "Moon-Over-the-Mountain"

Quilting stitches can outline the mountain and the moon. You can make several rows or just one outline row. The sky can be tufted. The little tufts will add the suggestion of stars in the sky.

Quilting and Tufting the Free-Form Landscape Appliqué

A line of quilting stitches can outline each mountain range and the sun. The quilting stitches can be used to add clouds in the sky and rays to the sun. Tufting over the sky area can again suggest stars.

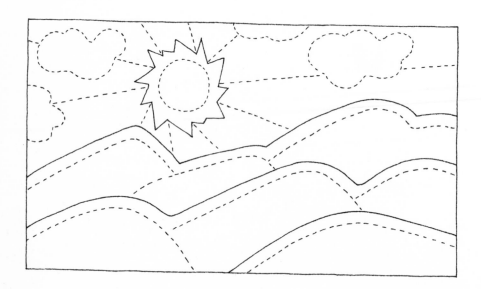

An appliquéd and quilted block. The farmer boy is appliquéd with fabric scraps; the head of the rake, house, and garden details are applied with permanent markers. Designed and sewn by Josie McKinley.

Les Riley adds a lot of patched detail to her landscapes and turns them into hangings, pillows, and handbags. Parts of the pillow at left are tufted for extra richness. Note how cleverly the quilting stitches are used to suggest waves for the water of the other scene.

Photo by Betty Pace Crawford, courtesy of artist.

Instant Quilting

This is easy and lots of fun to do. Each portion of the patchwork is made like a little pillow, stuffed and sewn as you go along. These stuffed quilts tend to be plump and bright and modern looking which is why we designed a warm and wintry sort of project to illustrate how it's done.

Skier's or Skater's Chest Warmer

Anyone who's ever gone up a chair lift to ski or sledded down a mountain on a bitter winter day will welcome this as a fashionable change from the plain old scarf.

Materials:

⅓ yard of felt, color A (for adults use ½ yard felt)

10″ square of felt, color B (for adults use two 10″ squares)

10″ square of felt, color C (for adults use two 10″ squares)

2 buttons

Stuffing

Skiers' or Skaters' Chest Warmer with appliqués of winter sports scenes cut from cotton prints. Joellen Sommer, designer-sewer.

Color A	Color B	Color A
Color C	Color A	Color C
Color B	Color C	Color B

← 9" →

How to Make It:

1. Cut two 9½″ squares out of paper (enlarge 3 or 4 inches for adults). Place carbon between the papers so you will have two patterns. Mark off nine rectangles as indicated in diagram.

2. Cut two felt patterns to match the paper pattern. Use color A for both.

3. Take the first color A patch and mark a 2½″ border along the sides and top. Cut out the center patch (see sketch) and put aside to use with other patches. You now have your neckband.

4. Cut the neckband in half at the top (see sketch). Sew two buttons on one side and cut slits for buttonholes in the other. Since felt does not fray it is not really necessary to outline the buttonholes with stitchery. However, making

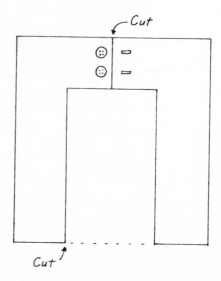

Cut

Cut

overhand stitches all around the buttonholes will reinforce them and also
add a decorative accent.

5. Pin each neckband to the top of the
other 9½″ felt square right sides facing. Baste and try on for size before going any further.

6. Cut felt patches to match the pattern.

7. If you want to appliqué your
patches, do so now.

8. Pin each patch to the piece with the
neckband attached. Sew the pockets in
place with running stitches, leaving the
top open. You will have nine open
pockets.

9. Stuff each pocket with scrap wool,
rags, or dacron and sew closed with a
running or overhand stitch. BE SURE
TO SEW THE NECKBANDS IN
WITH THE TWO CORNER
PATCHES.

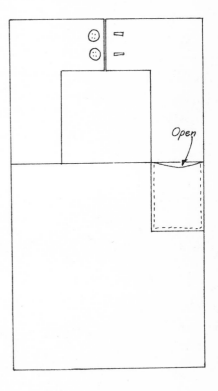

The puffed pillow technique can be
used to make a handsome Christmas
wreath. You will need approximately
½ a yard of fabric for a medium-sized
wreath. Cut a base of fabric with an 18″
diameter. Mark off a pattern of a

double row of patch pockets to go all around the wreath. The patch pockets should be cut so that they will extend beyond the wreath base so they can be stuffed into extra full and puffy pillows. For a really plump wreath, sew another layer of puff pockets to the underside of the wreath, using overhand stitches. A ribbon loop sewn to the top will serve as a hanger.

Puff Pillow Wreath by Josie McKinley.

Patchwork
Without
Sewing

Glued patchwork is the perfect answer for those who like designing but find sewing is not their thing. If you use smooth fabric such as cotton, brush the back with a mixture of half glue and half water. When the glues dries, the fabric will be as stiff and easy to cut as paper. The glue and water mixture brushed over the applied patches will hold them firmly in place. Your project can be wiped with a damp cloth.

Patchwork Puzzles

The idea for these patchwork puzzles was given to us by a talented woman named Bucky King. You'll find them great fun to make and great gifts to give.

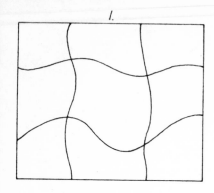

1.

Materials:

Cardboard, 20″ by 20″
An assortment of cotton print scraps
An assortment of felt scraps
White glue

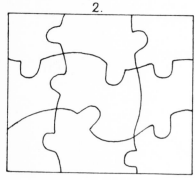

2.

How to Make It:

1. Draw two wavy vertical lines and two wavy horizontal lines on your cardboard. Use pencil so you can erase.

2. Erase some openings here and there and draw in "bumps" for the jigsaw pieces.

3. Cut out all nine pieces of cardboard.

4. Using your scraps of cotton cover each piece of cardboard with fabric, leaving extra fabric which can be glued to back of cardboard. Glue down smoothly, pressing out wrinkles.

5. Cut notches in the fabric so raw edges can be turned under and glued to the wrong side of the cardboard.

6. Draw outlines of each piece on felt. Cut out felt and glue to the back of the cardboard.

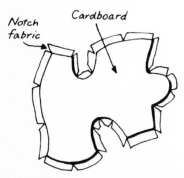

Notch fabric
Cardboard

Crazy Quilt
Wastepaper Basket

Here's your chance to use up every odd-shaped snippet of fabric you can find. By gluing instead of sewing, your crazy quilt pattern will be finished in no time. By "embroidering" your design with colored pencils or permanent markers, you will be creating an authentic crazy quilt look.

Materials:

Old wastepaper basket

Lots of scraps of cotton, denim, bits of lace, ribbons—

ANYTHING you have at hand, ANY SIZE

Half glue and half water solution

Permanent Magic Markers or colored pencils

How to Make It:

1. Prepare your fabrics by brushing the backs with glue and water mixture. Allow to dry. This step is optional but you will find your fabrics much easier to cut.

89

2. Start at the straight joining seam at the side of the basket and glue a straight-edged patch to this edge. It doesn't matter if you begin your design at the top or bottom of the basket.

3. Add a patch at a time, overlapping and cutting at random to form a pattern you like. This is free-form design, so let things happen spontaneously. Avoid using very large pieces. Your design will be more interesting and easier to handle if you use lots of small pieces.

4. When your basket is completely covered, add embroidery details with markers or colored pencils. Cross stitches and dots to simulate French knots would look fine.

5. Brush the entire design with an extra coat of glue and water.

Stuffed Appliqué Pictures

Since glue and water brushed onto the back of fabric will make it stiff enough to cut like paper, you can make all kinds of appliqué by cutting out designs from boldly printed fabrics, or by drawing your own on solid fabric. By stuffing your designs or portions of them as you glue them in place, you can achieve a quilted look.

Materials:
Fabric with bold print or plain fabric with a design drawn by you, using permanent washable markers or waterproof paints
Glue and water mixture
Sharp embroidery scissors
Polyester fill
Background of cloth-covered cardboard, a box, basket, etc.

How to Make It:
1. Brush the back of the print with half glue and water mixture. Let dry.
2. Cut the design carefully, as you would a paper doll.

3. Study your cut design to see if you want any areas to be raised up with stuffing. The eye of a fish, and/or its fins, the center of a flower would be good areas of a design to stuff.

4. With your fingers, mold the area to be stuffed, running your thumb from the center outward to shape and mold that part of the fabric. Apply glue to the fabric, not the stuffing, and press the stuffing in place.

5. Brush glue on the background and press your appliqué onto the background. Use your fingers or the back of a spoon to press down the edges of the appliqué.

More Ideas
and Projects

Patchwork Mobile

Patchwork mobiles made with geometric shapes can be given a richly textured look by layering three colors of felt and using reverse appliqué for one side and sewn-on appliqué for the other. The sample mobile is made with hexagons, all in one size. You could vary the size of each unit or use a combination of geometric shapes.

Materials:

Remnants of felt in three colors

Monofilament cord for stringing the mobile unit. This is a clear sturdy cord used for fishing reels and can be obtained in any finishing supply store and some hardware stores.

Dowel, wire, old hoop for suspending mobile

Small amount of stuffing (optional)

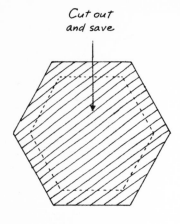

Cut out
and save

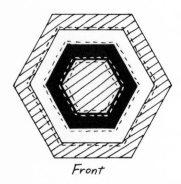

Front

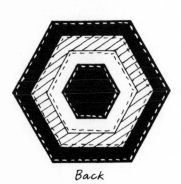

Back

How to Make It:

1. Make a template of the shape you want to use. If you make your mobile with different sizes or shapes, you will have to make a template for each size or shape.

2. To make each unit, outline the template on felt. Pin three colors of felt together and cut out. Your mobile should have at least five units so this step must be repeated at least five times.

3. Unpin the cut felt shapes. Mark off ½″ inside the top color and cut out the inside. Lay aside the inside piece.

4. Pin the second layer underneath the top layer and mark off another ½″ all around. Cut out this inside section and lay aside.

5. Pin the third layer underneath the top two. Mark off another ½″ all around. Cut out inside section and lay aside.

6. Turn your three-layered unit over and pin the largest cut-away center (from step 3) from the reverse appliqué side to the middle of the back.

7. Pin the other cutaway (in order of size) on top of the first unit. You can

94

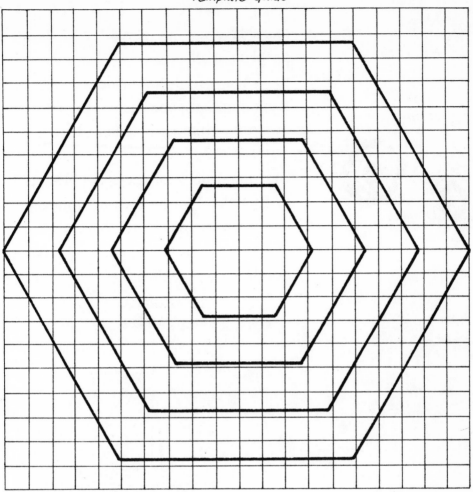

work a light layer of stuffing into the last unit or into all three.

8. With running stitch outline the layers, sewing through all the felt pieces. You will be going through three layers at the edge and stitching through six layers towards the middle. Felt is easy

95

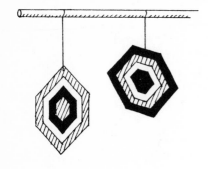

and soft to sew and you will find this no problem at all.

9. When you have made enough of these units, suspend them from a dowel or a round ring (see sketches).

Individual units of these double-appliqué patches can be used as ornaments or worn as pendants. Several units could also be sewn together to make a necklace.

Patchwork Turtle Pillow-Box

Soft sculpture is becoming an important part of the contemporary art scene.
Here's a chance to use patchwork to
turn a hard object into a soft sculpture
—trying out a new art form and recy-
cling all at one time.

Materials:

A small cigar box—the kind with a
paper-taped flip lid, approximately 5½"
by 7½"
Felt in 3 colors, ½ yard each
Stuffing—foam or polyester fill
Glue
Embroidery needle and yarn

How to Make It:

1. Enlarge the pattern for the turtle
shell. Each square in the diagram is
equal to one inch which means you can
enlarge the pattern by transferring it to
a grid ruled into one inch squares.
2. Cut out the squares marked 1-2-
3-4-5 in color A. Square 1 will measure
7 inches square and squares 2-3-4-5 will

Pattern Guide

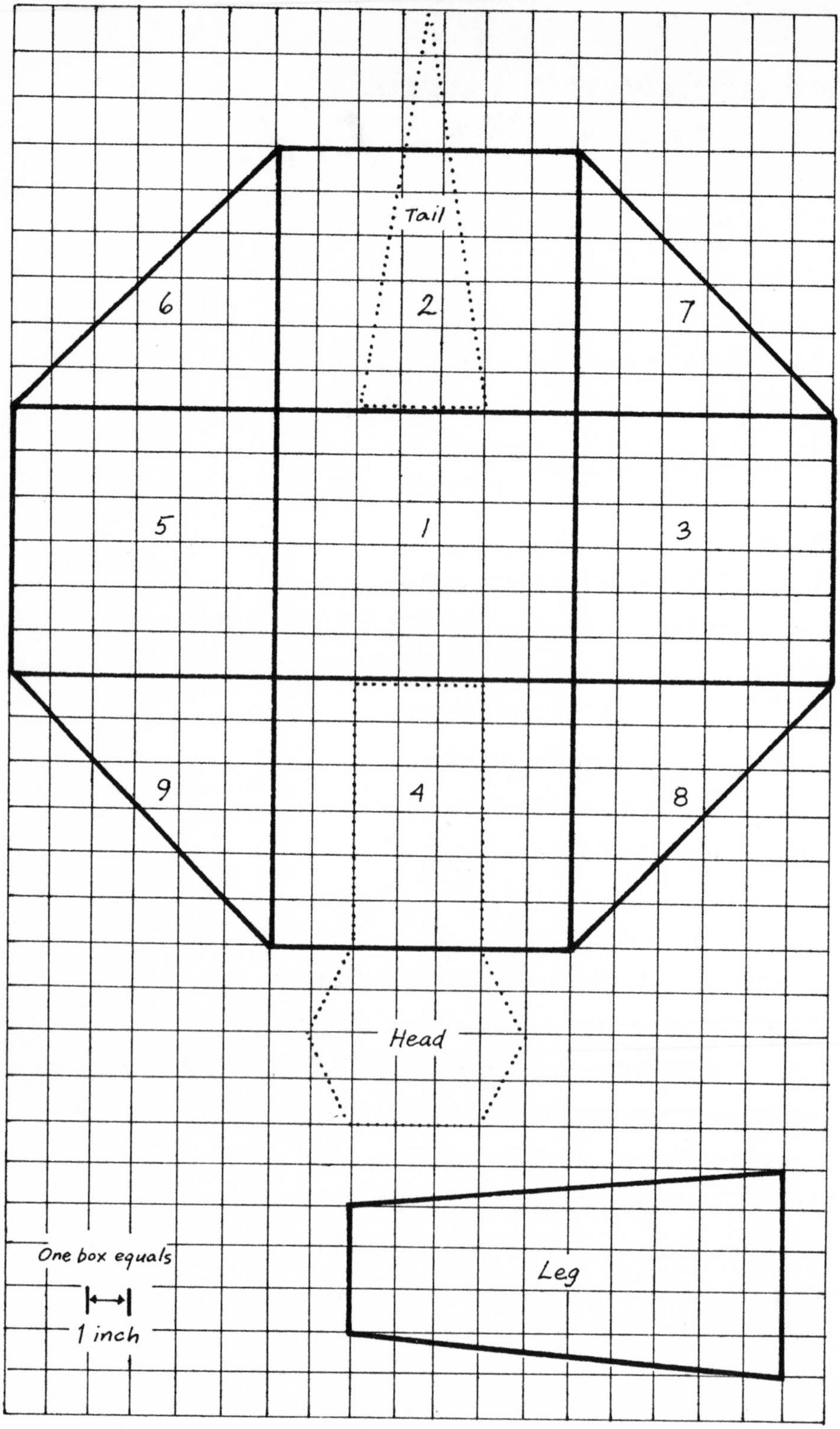
Tail
6
2
7
5
1
3
9
4
8
Head
Leg
One box equals
1 inch

measure 6 inches square each. Cut out the triangles in color B; each triangle will be half of a 6 inch square.

3. Sew patches together with overhand stitches in contrasting yarn which will provide extra decorative detail. The shell should be sewn in three rows of patches, in the following order: Row 1 combines patches 6, 2, 7; row 2 combines patches 5, 1 and 3; row 3 combines patches 9, 4 and 8.

4. After all the rows are patched, sew row 2 to row 1 and then sew row 3 to the combined rows 1-2. Use overhand stitches.

5. Pin your patched shell onto color C felt and cut the color C felt to match the patched shell for the underside of the turtle.

6. Sew all around the top and bottom of the shell with overhand stitches. When the two pieces are almost completely closed, stuff generously and complete sewing together. Put the shell aside.

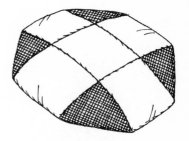

7. Cut a strip of felt to go all around the sides of the box. The strip should be slightly wider than the box. This will

Stuff

Glue
top
and
bottom
edges

make it possible to stuff the sides of the box, and change the box from a hard to a soft object. Glue the side strip in place, working stuffing into the center as you go along.

8. Enlarge the pattern for the turtle head, legs, and tail—still one inch to the box of a grid. Cut two pieces of felt for the head, eight leg pieces, and two tail pieces. Use color C for the head and leftovers from colors B and A for the legs and tail.

9. Sew the two head, two leg, and two tail pieces together as you did the top and bottom of the shell. Stuff each before closing completely.

Sew

10. Sew the head, legs, and tail to the bottom of the box, attaching to the stuffed areas at the sides, which will be easy to sew through. Center the head at the front, the tail at the back, and place the legs around the four corners.

11. Cut four strips of felt, about 3½ inches long each, from the leftovers (or use ribbons). Sew these to the underside of the turtle shell. Place the shell on top of the box lid and bring the sewn-on strips around the bottom of the lid. Glue them down tightly.

Glue
ribbons

The finishing touches: Cut an extra piece of felt to match the pattern of the lid and glue this over the inside of the box lid to hide the ribbons. Cut still another felt square and a felt strip to glue as a lining for the inside bottom and sides of the box. Glue one more patch of felt to the bottom of the box. Cut felt circles out of dark scraps and glue or sew to either side of the turtle's head for eyes.

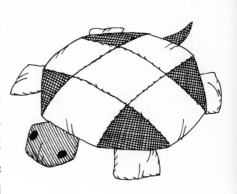

The finished sculpture can be used as a bed pillow or tabletop sculpture. The box can be used for trinkets.

Yo-Yo Necklace

Round fabric patches, ruffled together with basting stitches are called yo-yos in patchwork language. A small mirror put inside a yo-yo gives a very new look to this very old technique.

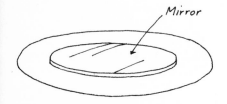
Mirror

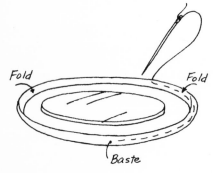
Fold   Fold
Baste

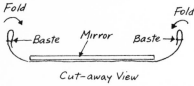
Fold   Fold
Baste   Mirror   Baste

Cut-away View

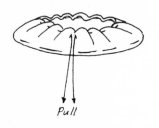
Pull

Materials:

Fabric scraps—cotton, silk or, if you don't want to turn under edges, felt
Small round mirrors or lids from small cans
Yarn for neckband

How to Make It:

1. Cut circles ¾ inch larger than the mirrors—½ inch larger if you use felt.
2. Make basting stitches all around the circle, folding the seam under as you baste.
3. Gently pull the basting stitches into a ruffle. Insert the mirror just before pulling the ruffle tight. Knot thread to finish.
4. Make as many mirrored yo-yos as you want. You can mix sizes. Lay them

out into an arrangement you like and tack them to each other with one or two stitches.

5. The neckband can be made from yarn braided into a chain, or you can use a regular neckchain from the jewelry or dime store.

You can, of course, make and use yo-yos without mirrors. They can be handsome accessories when they are made into belts or vests.

Lots of yo-yos can be sewn together to make a handsome vest. These yo-yos were made without inserting mirrors. Elyse Sommer, designer-sewer.

Appliqué Vest

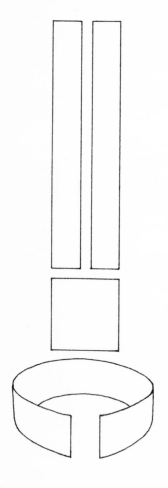

This vest requires no knowledge of clothing construction. Only square and rectangular shapes are used. The appeal is definitely unisex.

Materials:
Two cotton fabrics for top and lining, ½ yard (45″ width) each
Scraps for appliqué designs
Newspaper for pattern

How to Make It:
1. Make a paper pattern. Cut a 4″ wide strip of paper which measures around your waist. Make it a very snug fit since the vest will be worn open.
2. Next cut a 6″ to 8″ square for the back of the vest and tape or staple this to the top of the center of your strip.
3. For the shoulder straps, cut two 3″ wide straps which will go from the back square to the front of the waistband. Staple or tape the straps to the top of the square, then try on the vest to see how long your strips have to be to reach to the top of the waistband. Cut off the

excess straps and staple in place. You
now have a paper sample.

4. Cut fabric to match the paper patterns, but allow an extra ½″ all around
for seam allowance. Cut out a piece of
each fabric for each pattern piece.

5. Place your pattern pieces, the top
and the lining for each with the right
sides facing together and backstitch
along the seam line, all around three
sides of the waistband, back square,
and each of the straps. Turn each piece
right side out and finish sewing front to
back with overhand stitches.

6. Iron all your pieces but do not sew
together yet.

7. To appliqué the vest, let yourself go.
You can appliqué just the back square
or all of the parts. Make up your own
free-form appliqué designs like those
on the vest in the photograph or use
some of the appliqué ideas shown ear-
lier in the book. You could use the
moon-over-the-mountain appliqué for
the back square. The appliqués can be
outlined with quilting stitches.

8. After you have sewn your appliqués
in place, sew the back square to the

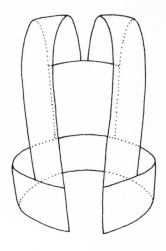

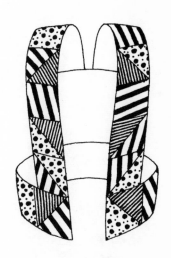

105

middle of the waistband. Then sew the straps to the top of the square and the top of the waistband. Use overhand stitches to attach the back square and the straps.

The vest can also be made by piecing the top fabric. If you make the top as a pieced patchwork, cut the patterns out in the lining fabric and piece the top portion to fit the paper shapes.

Free-form appliqué vest. Joellen Sommer, designer-sewer.

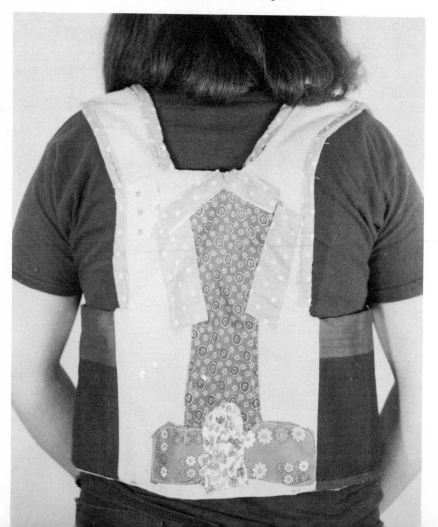

Patchwork Fabric Tennis Racket Cover

Unlike the appliquéd vest with its simple straight edges, a tennis racket cover is oval in shape. To work out a patchwork design so that the outside patches are cut exactly to the shape of this oval would be both difficult and time-consuming. Here's a great short-cut idea: Make one large piece of patchwork and then cut it to match the shape you want. This means that you will actually be cutting across some sewn seams so it's important to stitch the patches with very small close-together stitches. If any seams do open a bit, just sew across them to reinforce them.

Materials:

Scraps of sturdy fabric such as denim, sailcloth or pre-quilted cotton, enough to make ½ yard of patchwork fabric
Zipper—11 to 12″, or 11-12″ piece of Velcro

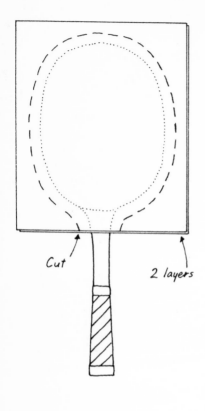

Cut

2 layers

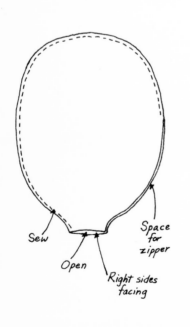

Sew

Open

Space
for
zipper

Right sides
facing

How to Make It:

1. Use your tennis racket as a template and make a paper pattern by tracing the racket and two inches of the handle on a double layer of newspaper. Enlarge this by ½″ all around to provide room for the racket.

2. Cut out the paper patterns. Staple them together, leaving an opening for zipper or velcro closing. Try the pattern on your racket to make sure it fits.

3. Make two pieces of patched fabric about an inch bigger all around than the paper patterns. You can use any patchwork pattern you want. Small squares, diamonds, hexagons are fine. Patchwork fabric also works out well in a random, overlapped crazy quilt mosaic. Whatever shapes you use, remember to use small, close-together stitches.

4. Pin your patchwork fabric to the paper patterns and cut it out. If any seam lines open up as you cut, make a few stitches to tack together.

5. Pin your two patchwork fabrics together, the right sides facing in. Leave the portion where the zipper will go unpinned.

108

6. Backstitch the pieces together. Sew in the zipper or velcro and turn right side out.

Once you've made this tennis racket cover, you can make patched fabric for any shape. If you like to sew clothing, you can now cut any pattern in your own handmade patchwork fabric.

Zipper

Patchwork and Appliqué Hassock

Here's your chance to practice both patchwork piecing and appliqué on a larger project.

Materials:

Five 16½″ squares of fabric. If you use felt you need 16″ squares since no seam allowance is necessary. Felt can be sewn with overhand stitches throughout.

Four prints to piece the 8-pointed star for the top square: four 4½″ squares in color A, two 4½″ squares in color B, one 4½″ square in color C and one 4½″ square in color D (4″ squares if using felt).

Scraps for appliqué to be sewn to the side squares

Shredded foam, a 16-inch foam block, or an inexpensive old hassock (16 inches is a fairly standard hassock size)

How to Make It:

1. Patch the top square into a star by cutting squares and triangles following

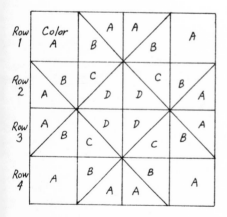

the sketch pattern. Use the template made for the Learn-By Doing Nine-Patch Pillow and the Triangle Patch-Pocket Tote Bag on pages 35 and 39. You will have four squares in color A, eight triangles in color A, eight triangles in color B, four triangles in Color C and four triangles in Color D.

Backstitch the triangles together to make squares. When the triangles are pieced you will have a total of 16 squares, laid out in four rows of four squares each.

Backstitch the four squares of each row together. Then backstitch row 2 to row 1, row 3 to rows 1-2 and row 4 to rows 1-2-3. This will complete your patched star top block.

2. Cut 16 8½″ squares of fabric (or 8″ squares of felt), to be used for the sides of the hassock. Of these four should be of color A, eight of color B, four of color D. Sew together in groups of four to match the diagram.

3. Cut out appliqué shapes in color C to decorate some or all of the side blocks. Small felt stars cut out in one piece, with perhaps a stuffed center,

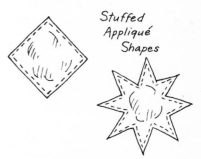

Stuffed
Appliqué
Shapes

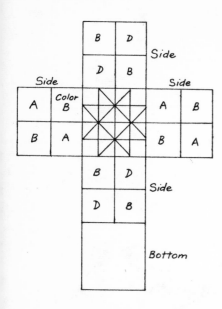

would carry through the top block design. Sew the appliqués in place with overhand or running stitches.

4. To turn the six blocks into a hassock, backstitch three of the side blocks to the top block to form a row of four, as shown in the sketch. Then backstitch the two remaining side blocks to the second block. With the right side blocks of the fabric facing IN proceed to backstitch the sides to one another so that a cube is formed. Attach all pieces, except the bottom, then turn your hassock inside out so the right sides are facing out again. Insert your stuffing and sew the bottom piece in place with overhand stitches. If felt is used, the entire hassock can be sewn together from the outside with overhand stitches.

use as a middle layer. Pin-baste all three pieces together, like a sandwich, and quilt stitch all around.

Checkerboard Rug. A mother-daughter cooperative project by the authors.

Patchworking in a Group

One of the nicest things about patchwork, appliqué, and quilting is that, depending upon your mood and what you are working on, you can enjoy these crafts alone or as a group activity. If large projects seem too overwhelming to do by yourself, why not follow in the footsteps of the patchworkers of times gone by?

When the pioneer women got together for the quilting bee or party, their purpose was not only to make the business of quilting easier but to bring some sociability into their hard and lonely lives. Husbands and children as well as the quilters enjoyed these parties. In addition to quilting bees where the finished quilt tops were quilted, there were also get-togethers to plan and design quilts as a group. A prospective wedding was a favorite occasion for a party. The group would decide on the size of each block and then each friend would make one block of the quilt and sign her name to her block in ink or stitchery. If someone moved away, friends would make a group quilt known as an album quilt. Sometimes there were surprise parties to honor some special person with a quilt which was then called a presentation quilt.

Today group or friendship quilting is once again popular and helping to spread the popularity and fun of the craft.

To celebrate New York's Bi-Centennial, some of the staff members of the Bi-Centennial Corporation organized a

New York City's Bicentennial Quilt.

Photo by George Batorfalvy/Jack Lipkins
Courtesy of the New York City Bicentennial Corporation.

neighborhood quilting bee workshop to bring together people of all ages to share their pride in their city by making one big patched quilt. An eight-year-old girl appliquéd her version of the Empire State Building to a long pieced patch. An eighty-year-old woman chose some neighborhood trees for her patch. Everybody contributed a patch. The result was not perfect by traditional patchwork standards, but it was exciting enough to inspire other neighborhood get-togethers and the original quilt traveled throughout the city, to be hung eventually in the Museum of the City of New York.

If you live in a big city, why not help plan a quilting party

Students of Miss Tempest Baker of the South Elementary School in Webster City, Iowa used stitchery to appliqué random-sized patches which were then sewn to a background fabric and mounted as hangings.

Photo courtesy of School Arts Magazine.

to personalize your neighborhood? If you live in a small town, you could get together a group to do a quilt about the town and its history.

Girl Scout and 4-H Groups can make a quilt to contribute to a local charity as a fund raiser—or perhaps have a party with another group, or a senior citizens group to see how well young and old can get along.

Patchwork is a fine class project. If your school has a wall that needs decorating, why not make a class banner?

Schools could exchange group quilts with other schools. This idea could even be carried out on an international basis. A quilt with appliqués of figures in different national costumes would be most appropriate here.

118

You don't need a large group to make quilting faster and more sociable. The Checkerboard Rug project on page 113 was a mother-daughter project made as a gift for the authors' son/brother. Each one made four of the eight rows of checkers. Each sewed one end and one side band.

When making group projects the results go far beyond what you actually see. If all the good feelings and happiness that get stitched into these projects could show, every friendship quilt would indeed be a masterpiece.

Children of Many Nations Quilt designed and made by Ruby Drake for *Quilters' Newsletter Magazine.*

Glossary

Album Quilt—Name given to a quilt made by a group, with each member making one quilted patch and signing it. Usually made for a person at some special occasion.

Appliqué—Pieces of fabric or pieced designs sewn to larger pieces. The word comes from the French word for applied. Modern appliqué includes stitched and painted designs as well as sewn fabrics.

Backing—This is the bottom of a quilt or the lining for a patchwork top.

Basting—Temporary fastening of fabrics. You can pin-baste or make very large, fast running stitches, or use both methods.

Batt or Batting—The middle layer of a quilt, used for warmth—once this was always cotton; today battings are available in dacron.

Binding—This refers to the finished edge of a quilt.

Block—Patchwork designs are made up of individual units known as blocks.

Crazy Quilt—A patchwork design made by the random combination of shapes and colors.

Friendship Quilt—This is a quilt made as a group project, like an Album Quilt.

Lap Quilting—Method of quilting together the layers of your work without special equipment such as a quilting frame. This is very popular today and best done with small projects or when large projects are quilted one block at a time.

Patchwork—Nowadays patchwork is often the catchall word to describe patchwork, quilting, AND appliqué. To be very specific, patchwork is the piecing together of a fabric with a number of small pieces.

Pin Basting—see basting.

Quilting—The final process in the making of a patchwork quilt. A top layer (the patchwork), a middle layer (the filler or batting), and a bottom layer (the lining or background fabric) are stitched together with small running stitches.

Quilting Bee—A party or get-together for the purpose of helping a friend quilt a finished patchwork design.

Quilt Top—The top layer of the quilt, usually the part which is patched and/or appliquéd.

Reverse Appliqué—A technique where several layers of fabric are sewn together, with portions of the design cut away from the top through to the back, so that the underneath prints show through. The San Blas Indians who perfected this technique are famous for their reverse appliqués or Molas.

Seam Allowance—The extra measurement allowed when cutting out fabric so that stitches are not made too close to the edge of the fabric which would cause it to unravel. The usual seam allowance is ¼″ to ⅜″.

Stuffed Appliqué—Third dimension added to appliqué by stuffing all or certain areas as the appliqué is stitched down.

Template—A pattern of stiff material used as a guide for making evenly cut fabric patches.

Tied Quilt—A method of attaching the layers of the quilt with lengths of yarn or thread tied in place and knotted.

Tufting—See tied quilts.

Yo-Yo—A type of patch made by puckering a circle of fabric into a ruffle.

Metric Conversion Chart

1 inch	— 2.54 centimeters
1 foot	— 0.3048 meter
1 yard	— 0.9144 meter
1 millimeter	— 0.0394 inch
1 centimeter	— 0.3937 inch
1 decimeter	— 3.937 inches
1 meter	— 1.094 yards

Sources of Supplies

Most of the materials and tools you need to do patchwork, appliqué, and quilting can be found around your own house or your local dime store or the notions counter of any department store. Here are some sources for buying things by mail.

DK Design
P.O. Box 7527
Oakland, Ca. 94601
Odd-sized dacron batting at discount prices. Send stamped addressed envelope for price sheet.

Home-Sew, Inc.
1825 West Market St.
Bethlehem, Pa. 18018
This company has a free 20-page illustrated catalogue picturing a variety of sewing supplies, including zippers and velcro.

Liberty Station
226 West Piedmont Street
Culpeper, Va. 22701
Quilt supplies, appliqué kits. Send for list.

Quilter's Newsletter
Box 394, Wheatridge, Colo. 80033
Templates, kits, books about quilting. Publishes a magazine called QUILTER'S NEWSLETTER which is a fine on-

going source of information about quilting methods and quilters. 75¢ per issue.

Sears Roebuck Company (look in your directory for address of store nearest you)
Batting, quilting frames

Stearns & Foster Co., Quilting Department
Cincinnati, Ohio 45215
Batting, patterns. Send 50¢ for catalogue.

For Further Reading

The following books are all available in inexpensive paper editions.

Coats & Clark Book #150, "100 Embroidery Stitches." Coats & Clark Corp., 430 Park Avenue, New York. 1964.

Ickis, Marguerite, "The Standard Book of Quilt Making and Collecting." New York, Dover Publications, Inc. 1959.

McKim, Ruby Short, "One Hundred and One Patchwork Patterns." New York, Dover Publications, Inc. 1962.

Sommer, Joellen, with Elyse Sommer, "Sew Your Own Accessories." New York, Lothrop, Lee and Shepard Co. 1972.

Index